AF335162

On Horseback

The many variations of sport on horseback, from pony trekking to rodeo and gymkhanas to show jumping, with exciting colour photographs of youngsters and the top international stars in action.

InterSport

On Horseback

Stephen White-Thomson

Colour photographs by All-Sport Limited

Wayland/Silver Burdett

InterSport

The world of international sport seen through the cameras of some of the world's greatest sports photographers, showing in action both children and the stars they admire.

Basketball	On Horseback
Cycling	Snow Sports
Golf	Soccer
Gymnastics	Swimming and Diving
Ice Sports	Tennis
Motorcycling	Track and Field

Frontispiece **One of Two** – Raimondo D'Inzeo of Italy. Both he and his brother Piero have been remarkably successful and consistent show-jumpers for many years.

First published in 1981 by Wayland Publishers Limited
49 Lansdowne Place, Hove, East Sussex BN3 1HF, England
© Copyright 1981 Wayland Publishers Limited
ISBN 0 85340 798 3

Published in the United States by Silver Burdett Company, Morristown, New Jersey
1981 Printing
ISBN 0 382 06516 6

Phototypeset by Trident Graphics Limited, Reigate, Surrey
Printed in Italy by G. Canale & C.S.p.A., Turin

Contents

Great moments

The partnership of man and horse produces some of the most spectacular moments in sport. The sight of two racehorses, galloping neck and neck, in a headlong dash for the finishing line in the Epsom Derby, is quite breathtaking. The grace and precision shown by the competitors in the Grand Prix Dressage is astonishing. The atmosphere in a major show jumping arena during a jump-off against the clock has a tension that is almost electric. Then there is the fast, thrilling sport of polo, the rough and tumble excitement of the rodeo and much more.

Of course, there are some moments which stand out above all others, the pinnacles of sporting achievement and drama. The great racehorse, *Red Rum*, produced such a moment in 1977, as he thundered home to win his third Grand National at Aintree in England. Since the Grand National is over 7 km (4½ miles) long, and the horses have to clear thirty fences, to win it even once is quite an achievement, but three times is almost unbelievable.

Lucinda Prior-Palmer's fourth win at the

Hat Trick Horse – *Red Rum* receives the applause of the Aintree crowd after his third Grand National victory.

Badminton Horse Trials was a feat of similar brilliance, as was David Broome's fourth victory in the King George V Gold Cup.

Another exciting moment came in the 1976 Olympics in Montreal, when the U.S.A. team, having taken the silver medal in the three previous Olympic three-day events, finally carried off the gold, beating West Germany into second place. They also took the individual gold and silver medals, through Edmund Coffin and John Plumb.

Clean Sweep – David Broome is the only rider to have won the King George V Gold Cup four times.

Leading Lady – Lucinda Prior-Palmer is undoubtedly the best lady three-day event rider in the world.

These are just a few examples. Whether you can ride or not, there are plenty of opportunities to witness great moments like these, either 'live', if you go along to watch the events, or on television. Once seen, they are seldom forgotten and, who knows, with lots of effort and determination you may even produce such moments yourself!

Starting out

Something to ride *on* is the first priority. For the majority of people, the most obvious starting-point is the riding school. Most leading countries boast a network of riding schools where tuition is given on hired ponies. These vary considerably in standard. There are few to match the schools at Saumur in France, Warendorf in Germany, or Gladstone in the U.S.A. In Britain it is advisable to contact the British Horse Society's 'Approvals' department; they are able to supply lists of approved riding schools.

The next step is to join one of the local branches of the Pony Club, which exists in many countries throughout the world. Before buying a pony, it is a good idea to seek the advice of the nearest Pony Club branch or the local riding school. Make sure you have the pony carefully looked over – otherwise you could end up buying a three-legged mule with a squint, and they don't show too well.

Once you are the proud owner of a pony, the door leading to all the excitement of equestrian sports opens a fraction. It needs a hard push to open it further. To enjoy riding

The First Hurdle – The gymkhana is the first real testing ground on the long road to success. This young rider is tackling it in fine style.

and to be successful needs hard work, pati-
ence and luck. But there's no harm in trying to
make the dream of riding at Hickstead or the
Madison Square Garden come true.

Good riders never stop learning. Instruc-
tion continues at rallies organized by the
Pony Club. Once you are confident in your
ability, you can graduate to the gymkhanas
which take place in most horse-loving
nations, and start your collection of colourful
rosettes. Many of today's top riders have, at
some stage, taken part in wildly enthusiastic
pony games, such as the Stepping Stone
Dash and the Potato Picking Scramble,
which are organized at many gymkhanas.

If you are not already a member of the
fast-growing fraternity of horse riders, one
reason may be lack of information about the
opportunities open to you. Another reason
will certainly be expense. Riding *is* a costly
occupation. But things are looking brighter
in Britain, where funds have always been a
problem. This is the result of the 'Riding
Foundation' which the British Horse Society
launched in 1977 to provide money for prom-
ising young riders. The BHS sends talent
spotters round to local gymkhanas, so make
sure you have some talent to be spotted.
Money is more readily available in the
U.S.A., because the United States Equestrian Team (America's wealthy sports foundation) enjoys charitable status and, there-
fore, does not have to pay so much tax.

Business and Pleasure – Each year more
than 150 teams enter for the Pony Club
Mounted Games Championship. Not only are
these games good training for both horse and
rider, but they are also great fun to compete in.

School Days – It is very important to learn the right way to ride. An approved riding school will be able to teach you all you want to know, whether it's how to ride side-saddle *(left)* or simply the art of trotting round the ring. *(above)*

The international scene

At the beginning of this century, there was a fear that the horse would be eclipsed by motor vehicles. But, in 1918, many people were keen to return to the glamour of the pre-war days – horses and all – and equestrianism has not looked back since. At first, the sport was dominated by the Military, and the competitions that took place were usually between rival cavalry regiments. Gradually civilians began to get into the game. Now millions of people ride and thousands take part in international competitions.

The growth of equestrian sport has made the smooth organization of international events essential. Just as the human body comprises many different pieces, and needs the head to control them, so the different equestrian sports need co-ordination or the whole movement becomes paralysed. This thought was uppermost in the mind of Baron du Teil, who founded the FEI (Fédération Equestre Internationale) in 1921. This is the brain and nervous system of the horse world. Today Prince Philip presides over a bureau

Polished Performance – The team which wins the most points in Nations Cups throughout the year is awarded the President's Cup.

of thirteen members from thirteen different countries. Their influence and efficiency belies any superstition that thirteen is an unlucky number.

The sixty or so members of this international federation each have their own national federations, which are like blood brothers to the FEI. The American H.Q. is in New York, and the British Equestrian Federation has its home at Kenilworth. Normally, they are closely linked with the country's national equestrian centres, which act as the focus for all equestrian activities. Sweden has its centre at Strömsholm, Germany at Warendorf, while Spain's heart is at the Club de Campo in Madrid.

It is the FEI's responsibility to create and supervise international competitions. They are heavily involved with the Olympics every four years, the World Championships every four years (between the Olympics), and the European Championships every two years. They also have a hand in organizing Nations Cup championships throughout the year. The country that wins the most points in these events wins the President's Cup. Since 1965, this has been won the most times by Britain.

The Organizer – Prince Philip, President of the Bureau of the FEI, guides a team of bays round the obstacle course at the Royal Windsor Horse Show.

Show jumping

Show jumping is the most popular of all the equestrian sports, and receives most attention from the media. It has an immediate appeal on the television screen, which can capture most, if not all, of the drama and excitement of riders urging their mounts over colourful obstacles. Most of these obstacles are much higher than the average person. It is also the most lucrative event, and nowadays top-class horses are worth over £50,000 ($110,000).

As a special set of fences is designed and built for each competition, show jumping has been described as a test in which the course designer is the examiner and the competitors are the examinees. There is no doubt that it takes great courage and skill to tackle the Derby Bank at Hickstead, or the great 2.13 m (7 ft) wall at Amsterdam. The course at Hamburg was so difficult that there were no clear rounds in fifteen years from 1929 to 1944. Horse and rider must act as one unit, twisting and turning sharply to meet the fences head on, and take off at just the right moment. Jumping a fraction of a second too

The Slippery Slope – Judy Crago and *Bouncer* descend the Derby Bank at Hickstead, one of the most difficult obstacles in the world of show jumping.

early or too late can lead to disaster. Alwin Schockemöhle on *Warwick Rex*, and Eddie Macken on *Kerrygold*, are perfect examples of this essential teamwork.

A competition which tests jumping ability alone is called a 'puissance'. These are especially exciting when competitors score equal points in the early rounds. They then have to 'jump-off' against each other, the fences becoming progressively more difficult until,

Top Teams – At international level, a good understanding between horse and rider is absolutely vital. Alwin Schockemöhle *(above)* on *Warwick Rex* and Eddie Macken on *Kerrygold (right)* are fine examples of this.

ERRES

by the survival of the fittest, a winner emerges. Most show jumping competitions have a time element, and it is tremendously exciting to see horses race against the clock.

The leading show jumping nations are Germany, Italy, the U.S.A. and Britain. Many others such as Canada, Switzerland, Holland, Belgium and Ireland all produce very good competitors. The Germans, on their powerful Hanoverian horses, have always enjoyed success at an international level, with men like Hans Winkler and Hendrik Snoek featuring among the great

Riding High – Hans Winkler was in the German show jumping team at every Olympic Games from 1956 to 1976, during which time they won four gold medals, one silver and one bronze.

Getting Closer – Harvey Smith keeps an eye on the wall as *Sanyo Krakatoa* takes off.

names. Italy has been brilliantly represented by the D'Inzeo brothers. Frank Chapot and Bill Steinkraus regularly star in the show jumping hall of fame for America, benefiting from the expert training of Bert de Nemethy. David Broome, Caroline Bradley and Harvey Smith have all ridden for Britain with great success.

In the course of a year, this fraternity of show jumpers will travel to horse shows all over the world. They will take part in competitions in New York, Toronto, Hamburg, Palermo and London, to name but a few.

Eventing

'Eventing', 'Horse Trials', 'The Military', and 'Le Concours Complet' are different names given to the same competition, which is designed to test the all-round ability of horse and rider. The most popular is the three-day event. This is divided into three phases – dressage, cross country, and show jumping – which test basic training, stamina and accuracy. Courage is a vital element of success. Neither horse nor rider should get 'spooked' at the obstacles. 'Throw your heart over first' is a piece of advice often given to novices during the cross country part of the competition, which sees more than its fair share of thrills and spills.

The three-day event was first introduced into the Olympic Games at Stockholm in 1912. As well as the Olympic Games, there are now the Pan-American games and the World and European Championships, which are held for juniors too, giving fourteen- to eighteen-year-olds invaluable experience of international competition. Sweden, Holland, Germany, the U.S.A. and Britain have taken it in turns to dominate the international

Medals for Meade – Richard Meade won Olympic three-day event golds in Mexico and Munich, and he also won at Badminton in 1970.

eventing scene. Bruce Davidson, an American, won the World Championship in 1978 on *Night Tango*. Fellow Americans Mike Plumb and Edmund Coffin have enjoyed great success in recent years under the direction of Jack Le Goff, their team trainer. Britain's riding ace, Richard Meade, has won two Olympic golds on *Cornishman V* in Mexico in 1968, and *Laurieston* at Munich in 1972. But the leading equestrian nations do not always have things their own way, for there have been individual winners from many other countries – for example, Marian Babirecki from Poland and Alexander Evdokimov of the Soviet Union have both won medals in European competitions.

Dressage

Most countries, with Germany as the notable exception, are suspicious of dressage. Some regard it as more of a science than a sport, others think it is little more than a circus act. True, it is not as full-blooded or exciting as the cross country or show jumping, but it has a fascination all of its own. There are several grades of competition, ranging from the most basic tests to the Grand Prix Special. In the latter, horses and riders perform

Best of British – Jennie Loriston-Clarke is the most successful British rider on the dressage scene. *(left)*

Smooth Manoeuvres – Any change of speed or step must be achieved smoothly and rhythmically. *(above)*

the most remarkable feats of controlled grace. The skills shown by the world-famous white Lippizaners of the Spanish riding school in Vienna are magnificent examples of this. The grace, power and precision of their movements are like those of a ballet dancer. One of the best-known movements is the 'capriole', when the horse leaps off the ground and kicks violently with both hind legs. This action is derived from a battle technique used by knights in the Middle Ages to get rid of any infantrymen attacking from behind.

International dressage contests take place in the Olympic Games, and there are also the World Dressage Championships. Christine Stuckelberger of Switzerland on *Granat* is the most consistently successful dressage rider. America's Hilda Gurney on *Keen*, and Britain's Jennie Loriston-Clarke on *Dutch Courage*, have both done well for their respective countries.

The dressage phase of the three-day event is not designed to test such intricate skills. It has the simpler task of testing the horse's co-ordination, training, and obedience to the will of its rider. This is achieved by putting horse and rider through a series of movements performed at the walk, trot and canter. Judges mark each section separately, as they do in skating. The rider with the fewest penalty points goes through to the next round in the lead.

In Control – The dressage phase of a three-day event is designed to test the horses' basic training and obedience. The most intricate skills are tested in the Olympic Games and the World Championships.

Cross country

Cross country is the most gruelling phase of the three-day event. It is also the most exhilarating part of the event for both horse and rider – and often for the spectators too, since they sometimes witness spectacular falls.

The cross country section of a three-day event normally has four parts. The first of these is a short roads and tracks phase. There is then a 3-km (2-mile) steeplechase course, which must be taken at full gallop. This is followed by a longer roads and tracks phase, over perhaps 9–11 km (6–7 miles), which is taken at a slightly slower pace than the first phase. Finally there is the cross country course itself, which is generally between 5 and 7 km (3 and 4½ miles) long. There are usually thirty or more obstacles, which can be stone walls, huge logs, water obstacles, solid wooden fences, steep banks or combinations of these.

Timing has to be perfect. To go too fast often results in a fall and heavy time penalties. But to travel too slowly also invites time penalties, so the rider must judge his or her speed to perfection. This is not always easy after a long, tiring ride over obstacles which, according to Colonel Frank Wheldon, course-builder and director of Badminton, are designed to 'frighten the rider'. For this reason, falls are not uncommon.

In the Swim – Water is just one of the many obstacles encountered in the cross country section. *(above)*

Nose Dive – Jane Winter comes unstuck at Goodwood, England. Perhaps the horse was thirsty! *(right)*

17
B

The Final Phase – After the dressage and the cross country, the three-day event is completed by a show jumping competition. *(above)*

Show jumping

On the third day, when both horse and rider are ready for a long rest, the show jumping section of the contest puts their stamina to the severest test. The course is easier than in a normal show jumping competition, and is designed to see how strong and sure-footed the horse is after its strenuous exertion of the previous two days.

You have to be a Jack – or Jill – of all trades to win a three-day event. It is certainly the most physically demanding of all the equestrian sports and, until recently, it was thought to be too tough for women. In the last few years, however, women like Princess Anne and Lucinda Prior-Palmer have proved that they are as tough and successful as the men in this gruelling sport.

Up and Over – The fences used for the final section of a three-day event are not as difficult as those in a normal show jumping competition. *(below)*

Driving

During the Second World War, when there was a shortage of fuel for cars, people rediscovered traps and carriages where they had lain in garages and back yards, gathering dust and cobwebs over the years. They were cleaned, attached to horses by brightly-polished leather harnesses, and used for travelling about the countryside cheaply. By the time the war finished, many people had acquired the taste for driving in harness, and had developed great pride in the appearance of their carriages. It was natural that they should want to show them.

In Britain, a few shows organized driving classes, but not enough to ensure a healthy future. But, in 1957, a decisive development guaranteed that the sport would take off in Britain. The British Driving Society was formed. There are now 3000 members of this society, and its numbers increase daily. They can attend a hundred meetings each year, organized on a regional basis to overcome the obvious difficulties of transporting the vehicles from place to place.

Great Britain has finally caught up with

Driving Force – Sir John Miller's team charges through the water during a cross country driving event. *(above)*

This is the Life! – Driving through the countryside behind a team of four trotting ponies must be one of the best ways to travel. *(right)*

Germany, where driving has long been part of the sporting scene. Together, these countries have helped to promote and develop the sport in the U.S.A. and Canada. At the Royal Windsor Horse Show in 1970, the first of many international competitions was held. As in the three-day event, it was organized into three phases, with a presentation and dressage phase, a marathon and an obstacle race. German, Hungarian, Dutch and British competitors have featured in the medal tables most often.

Driving is a sport that is taken very seriously by those who compete, but it still has an air of romantic excitement about it. When you see a carriage tearing across country, pulled by four sweating, straining horses, it reminds you of centuries gone by, when the horse was the only form of transport. At any moment you expect a highwayman to ride out of the trees and demand 'your money or your life'. Even the names of the vehicles, like the 'Spindleback', the 'Parisienne Wagonette' or the 'Sulky', conjure up a great charm.

There can be little doubt that driving, once the baby of the equestrian scene, has finally come of age.

Water Wheels – Christian Iseli of Switzerland and his team of geldings surge through a water obstacle in Windsor Home Park.

Long-distance riding

You don't have to be an experienced rider to go pony trekking, and this is the way most youngsters get their first ride. Trekking holidays have a long pedigree in South America and the U.S.A., where it is possible to trek right down into the Grand Canyon and many other exciting places. They have recently become popular in Britain, where the English Riding Holiday and Trekking Association gives good advice on the best trekking centres and makes sure you get value for money. The recipe for the success of trekking is the opportunity it gives to learn to ride in beautiful countryside, while the horses' legs do the work!

Another popular form of long-distance riding is the team cross country event, the brainchild of Douglas Bunn, director of Hickstead. He first put his ideas into practice in 1974. Teams of five competed on a 4-km (2½-mile) course over twenty to twenty-five fences. The time of the fourth past the post was taken as the time for the whole team, so

The Scenic Route – A group of trekkers sample the beautiful scenery of the Rocky Mountains.

it did not matter if the last rider failed to finish. The tactic was for the most experienced rider to blaze a trail which the others could follow. It was an instant success. The format remains unchanged except for a new rule, introduced in 1978, which insists that the team jumps in unison over two fences of the course, which makes it a more genuine team effort. This new sport, which is perfectly suited to the English countryside, has spread like wildfire, and it seems that nothing will quench the flames.

The sport of long-distance riding itself has been going on for many years in the rugged terrain of the U.S.A. and Australia. The most coveted prize in the U.S.A. is the Trevis Cup, which goes to the winner of the 160-km (100-mile) ride, held in the memory of the famous Wells Fargo stagecoach service. The 'Tom Quilty' ride, through the Blue Mountains of New South Wales, is the toughest on the Australian calendar. In 1966 it was won by Gabriel Stecher, who rode an Arab stallion, *Shalawi*, bareback over the 160-km (100-mile) course. There is nothing so severe in Britain, where the sport is in its infancy, but the 120-km (75-mile) Golden Horseshoe ride on Exmoor is testing to both horse and rider. The sport seems assured of a great future, with membership increasing each year. An international long-distance rally in Europe is now a regular feature of the equestrian calendar.

Relaxing Rides – The great thing about trekking is that you can admire the view without having to do the work!

Point-to-point and National Hunt

Point-to-points are races for amateurs organized by most Fox Hunts throughout Britain. In the beginning, the races were held from a certain point to the nearest church tower, which is why they are also called steeplechases. They soon moved onto the local farmers' land, much to the relief of the parish priest, and are now held on oval tracks over twenty or so brushwood fences. The horses, which must have a certificate to prove that they have been 'well and truly' hunted, race over nearly 6.5 km (4 miles). The 200 fixtures, held over 120 courses in the short season from February to May, are watched by thousands of people for whom point-to-pointing is a marvellous social, as well as sporting, occasion. It is still an amateur sport, and the prize money, for those lucky enough to win, only just covers the owners' expenses.

The same is not true of the National Hunt which is a competition like the point-to-point. This sport is for professionals, and a great deal of money is involved. The most

Working Up an Appetite – Apprentice jockeys take their horses out for an early-morning gallop before breakfast. *(above)*

On Their Last Legs – The three leaders clear the last fence in the Beaufort point-to-point Ladies Open. Not much further to go! *(right)*

Blue Riband for *Red Rum* – The hero of the Grand National takes a breather after his third victory in what is probably the toughest National Hunt race in the world. *(above)*

famous race in the world, the Grand National at Aintree, England, was started in 1839. It is a difficult course with big fences like Beechers' Brook taking a heavy toll on the thirty-five starters, and seldom more than ten finish! It has been the scene of many great triumphs for horses like *Arkle*, *Mill Reef* and, more recently, *Red Rum*. National Hunt racing is now a flourishing sport in many parts of the world. The Colonial Cup and the Maryland Hunt Cup are

An Unsettling Experience – John Burke parts company with *Royal Frolic* in the Cheltenham Gold Cup in England. *(right)*

The High Jump – Huge fences like 'The Chair' and 'Beecher's' produce many falls in the Grand National at Aintree. This unseated jockey simply has to keep his head down and hope for the best while he waits for the rest of the horses to jump.

two of the major races in America, and countries like France, Czechoslovakia and New Zealand all have their own 'Grand National' races.

To win a great National Hunt race is the ambition of many youngsters. It is an ambition that few realize – but someone has to win the races of the future. If you are keen to become a jockey, you should write to a stable and ask for a job. It is vital that you like

Neck and Neck – Two horses battle it out during a point-to-point race. The horses used in these races are getting better all 'the time, and it is not unusual to see an ex-Grand National horse running in a point-to-point.

horses, don't mind hard work for little pay, and have small feet, because that gives some idea of how big you will grow! After a while, if you are doing well, the owner of the stable may let you ride a hack and then, perhaps, try you on a racehorse on an early morning ride. If you show promise, the trainer will give you a chance on a lightweight horse in a handicap. Your future from then on depends on your success.

Flat racing

It is impossible to say when the first horse-race took place. All we know is that it was a long time ago. Cossacks have raced against each other on the steppes of Russia for hundreds of years, and the Greeks and Romans almost certainly organized horse-races in bygone centuries. Mention is often made of racing during the Middle Ages.

The Gold Cup at Newmarket in England was first contested in 1634 and the first English Derby was run in 1780. Two hundred years later, the 1980 Derby was watched by over 300,000 people on the beautiful Epsom course. £30 million ($70 million) was spent on the race in bets – gambling has always been popular, and many fortunes have been won and lost on the major races.

The 1980 English Derby was won by Willie Carson on *Henbit*, which was the jockey's second successive Derby victory. Lester Piggot on *Monteverdi* was not placed that year, and so was unable to claim his ninth Derby win.

Apart from the Derby, the four other Classic races in England are the 2000 and the 1000 Guineas (both run at Newmarket),

The Jewel in the Crown – The Epsom Derby is the top event in the English flat racing calendar. The race is watched by thousands of people on the course, and by millions more on television.

American Classic – The Kentucky Derby is one of the three major races in the U.S.A. It is held in early May each year on the Churchill Downs track. Unlike British racecourses, the track is made of turf covered with sand.

the Oaks at Epsom and the St Leger at Doncaster. *Nijinsky*, one of the greatest racehorses of all time, won the Triple Crown of the Derby, St Leger and 2000 Guineas.

Other countries have followed Britain's example and today there is horse-racing in Australia, New Zealand, South Africa, Canada, Ireland, France, Italy, Germany, the U.S.A., South America, Hong Kong and many other countries. Each country has its

Winning Combination – Willie Carson and *Henbit*, 1980 Epsom Derby winners.

own great races. Some of the better known are the French Prix de l'Arc de Triomphe, the Kentucky Derby in America, and the Melbourne Cup in Australia, always the scene of frenzied excitement. It is difficult to disagree with the punters, who think that there are few more thrilling sights in the world than to watch sleek thoroughbreds racing flat out against each other, straining every muscle to get past the post first.

Polo

Polo is claimed, by those who play, to be the most exciting and dramatic game in the world, and it is certainly one of the fastest. It originated in Persia, China and Northern India centuries ago. The game survived in small peaceful valleys in Northern India, where it was discovered by British Cavalry officers and adopted with relish. They found that the speed and exhilaration of the game served two purposes: it was excellent sport, and marvellous training.

They founded clubs in India and, eventually, in England. The first match played in England was in 1871 at Hounslow, between two Cavalry regiments. The Hurlingham Club – the centre of polo in Britain – was founded soon afterwards. The game was introduced into America in the late 1870s and, by 1914, was known all over the world. Wherever there was plenty of sun, wide open spaces and a good supply of healthy horses, polo was played.

The object of the game is to score as many goals as possible. There are two posts to mark the goal at either end of the pitch, and

In Full Swing – This polo player is about to let go with an off-side backhander, in order to drive the ball away from his own goal. The ball is made of solid wood, and so the horses' legs are protected with boots or bandages.

the hard ball is driven at lightning speed with a stick wielded by the rider. It is similar to hockey on horseback. The ponies do so much galloping around and charging into opponents' horses, that they are changed after each 'chukka', which lasts seven-and-a-half minutes. They have to be changed or they would drop dead from exhaustion! Tournaments seldom last longer than six chukkas. As in golf, there is a handicap system which allows less experienced teams to play good ones, and still do well.

Despite the great expense it involves, polo is played in many different countries, from Hawaii to the United Arab Republic. The leading nations are the U.S.A., Argentina and Britain, and they compete for the Westchester Cup (Britain v. America) and the Cup of the Americas (Argentina v. America). Polo was also included in the Olympic Games for a while, but was dropped after the Berlin Olympics in 1936. So few teams took part that each team was guaranteed a medal!

Although the number of people who play is small, the popularity of the sport is not declining. It is due to the enthusiasm of Prince Philip and Prince Charles that polo thrives in England, and their efforts have been helped by the recent offer from Pony Clubs to hire out ponies to keen polo-playing members for a small sum of money. Because of this, polo is no longer solely a rich man's sport. So why not give it a try?

Early Start – It is now easier for youngsters to participate in the sport of polo, thanks to the Pony Club's offer to loan ponies to their members. *(above)*

That's Mine! – Two opposing players fight for possession of the ball during the Queen's Cup Final. *(right)*

SLADMORE

Unusual equestrian sports

You can find horses taking part in many weird and wonderful sports all over the world. In the alpine countries, horses with skiers harnessed behind them race against each other through the ice and snow. This sport is called ski-joring. The skier needs great courage, especially round corners when the horses are doing a full gallop. 'Father Christmas' ice-sled races are also immensely popular, with teams of horses pulling a chariot on skis, like Ben Hur on ice! In a different climate, in the burning heat of a Spanish bull ring, picadors ride horses and help the matador to fight the bull.

North America is the scene of many exciting sports involving horses, and the tradition of the cowboys of the Wild West is kept alive. The biggest Wild West Show is the Calgary Stampede in Western Canada. In July each year, more than a million visitors flood into the town to relive those exciting, adventurous days of old. For nine days, the city becomes an old frontier town, filled with cowboys and throbbing with excitement. All the old cowboy tricks and skills are now sport. There is

Hang on to Your Hats! – Chuck-wagon racing is one of the spectacular events to be seen at the Calgary Stampede. The wagons thunder along at breakneck speed leaving trails of dust behind them, while thousands of spectators cheer on their favourites.

rodeo, cutting, chuck-wagon racing, lassoing
of steer and many other spectacular displays.

From all over the country, rodeo riders
come to Calgary and try to win big prizes by
staying in the saddle on top of bucking bron-
cos. Nine times out of ten the horse wins,
catapulting its rider on to the ground as it
twists, bucks, rears and jack-knifes – called
'sunfishing' in the trade.

In the sport of 'cutting', the cutting horse

Round 'Em Up – The events of the Calgary
Stampede date back to the old Wild West days.
The art of lassoing a steer is the same as it
was then, and you still win some and lose
some. *(above and right)*

Still on Top . . . But only just. The bucking bronco is a feature of almost every North American horse show, and it's always a great favourite with the crowds.

acts like a sheepdog, separating a steer from its herd and keeping it apart from the rest of the cattle, which tests the horses' skill to the limit.

Chuck-wagon racing began when cowboys finished their cattle round-up. In their wagons, they would race one another across the prairies to the luxuries of the bars and dance halls in town. In the fiercely contested

Man Overboard! – The rider seems to be coming off second best in this encounter with his four-legged friend.

races at Calgary, all is a blur of horses, riders and wagons. The shouts of the crowd are lost in the welter of dust and the thunder of hooves and wagon wheels.

Although the Calgary Stampede is the greatest show of its kind on earth, it is possible to see most of these Wild West sports at shows all over Canada, the U.S.A., Australia and New Zealand.

Index

All pictures by All-Sport Photographic Ltd., except on pages 10, 13, 14, 15, 23, 24, 40 and 45 (Bob Langrish), pages 30, 43 and 49 (Pony and Light Horse), page 52 (Carl Byoir) and page 59 (Alberta Government).